LEARNING THROUGH PLAY

Summary Publications in the Johnson & Johnson Baby
Products Company Pediatric Round Table Series:

Maternal Attachment and Mothering Disorders:
A Round Table

Edited by Marshall H. Klaus, M.D.,
Treville Leger and
Mary Anne Trause, Ph.D.

Social Responsiveness of Infants

Edited by Evelyn B. Thoman, Ph.D.
and Sharland Trotter

Learning Through Play

By Paul Chance, Ph.D.

LEARNING THROUGH PLAY

by Paul Chance, Ph.D.

*Summary of a Pediatric Round Table
Cochaired by Brian Sutton-Smith, Ph.D.
and Richard Chase, M.D.*

Foreword by
Urie Bronfenbrenner, Ph.D.

Sponsored by

Johnson & Johnson

BABY PRODUCTS COMPANY

Gardner Press, Inc.
19 Union Square West
New York 10003

Library of Congress Cataloging in Publication Data

Chance, Paul.
  Learning through play.

  (Johnson & Johnson Baby Products Company pediatric
round table series; 3)
  Summarizes the proceedings of the Round Table on Play
and Learning, held March 13-16, 1977, in New Orleans.
  Bibliography: p.
  1. Play. 2. Children—Language.   3. Educational
games.   I. Johnson & Johnson Baby Products Company.
II. Round Table on Play and Learning, New Orleans,
1977. III. Title. IV. Series: Johnson & Johnson Baby
Products Company. Johnson & Johnson Baby Products
Company pediatric round table series ; 3.
LB1137.C43   155.4'18   79-4549
ISBN 0-931562-02-3

Printed in the United States of America

This book is dedicated to the researchers, teachers, parents, health care professionals and others who, directly or indirectly, help children learn through play.

CONTENTS

PARTICIPANTS

WILLIAM H.BORTREE
Manager, Child Development Products
Johnson & Johnson Baby Products Company
220 Centennial Avenue
Piscataway, NJ 08854

RICHARD ALLEN CHASE, M.D.
Associate Professor, Psychiatry & Behavioral Sciences
The Johns Hopkins University School of Medicine
Baltimore, MD 21218

PAUL CHANCE, Ph.D.
Department of Psychology
California State University
San Luis Obispo, CA 93407

ROBERTA R. COLLARD, Ph.D.
Associate Professor, School of Education
University of Massachusetts
Amherst, MA 01003

MIHALY CSIKSZENTMIHALYI, Ph.D.
Professor, Committee on Human Development
University of Chicago
5730 South Woodlawn Avenue
Chicago, IL 60637

MICHAEL ELLIS, Ph.D.
Head, Department of Physical Education
University of Oregon
University Avenue
Eugene, OR 97403

GRETA FEIN, Ph.D.
Professor, Child Development and
Director, Child Development Research
The Merrill Palmer Institute
71 East Ferry Avenue
Detroit, MI 48202

HOWARD GARDNER, Ph.D.
Codirector, Harvard Project Zero
Research Psychologist, Veterans Administration Hospital
Psychology Service
150 South Huntington Avenue
Boston, MA 02130

CATHERINE GARVEY, Ph.D.
Professor, Department of Psychology
The Johns Hopkins University
Charles & 34th Streets
Baltimore, MD 21218

DALE HAY, Ph.D.
Assistant Professor, Department of Psychology
State University of New York at Stony Brook
Stony Brook, Long Island, NY 11794

CORINNE HUTT, Ph.D.
Department of Psychology
University of Keele
Keele, Staffordshire, England

GAVIN HILDICK-SMITH, M.D.
Corporate Director, Medical Affairs
Johnson & Johnson Research
501 George Street
New Brunswick, NJ 08903

JERRY W. HOBSON
Product Director
Johnson & Johnson Baby Products Company
220 Centennial Avenue
Piscataway, NJ 08854

BARBARA KIRSCHENBLATT-GIMBLETT, Ph.D.
Associate Professor, Department of Folklore & Folklife
University of Pennsylvania
415 Logan Hall
Philadelphia, PA 19104

MICHAEL LEWIS, Ph.D.
Professor and Director
Institute for the Study of Exceptional Children
Educational Testing Service
Princeton, NJ 08541

LOIS F. LUNIN, M.S.
Vice President
Herner & Company
2100 M Street, N.W.
Washington, DC 20037

ROBERT McCALL, Ph.D.
Fellow
Boys Town Center for the Study of Youth Development
Boys Town, NB 68010

CANDACE NEALE-MAY, R.N., M.S.
Assistant Director, Professional Relations
Johnson & Johnson Baby Products Company
501 George Street
New Brunswick, NJ 08903

STEVEN SAWCHUK, M.D.
Director, Medical Services and
Chairman, Institute for Pediatric Service
Johnson & Johnson Baby Products Company
220 Centennial Avenue
Piscataway, NJ 08854

THOMAS R. SHULTZ, Ph.D.
Associate Professor, Department of Psychology
McGill University
1205 McGregor Avenue
Montreal, Quebec, Canada H3A 1B1

HELEN SCHWARTZMAN, Ph.D.
Research Scientist, Institute for Juvenile Research
1140 South Paulina Street
Chicago, IL 60612

DOROTHY SINGER, Ed.D.
Codirector, Family Television Research & Consultation Center
Research Affiliate, Yale Child Study Center
Professor, Department of Psychology
Yale University
Box 11A, Yale Station
New Haven, CT 06520

JEROME SINGER, Ph.D.
Codirector, Family Television Research & Consultation Center
Director, Clinical Psychology Training Program
Professor, Department of Psychology
Yale University
Box 11A, Yale Station
New Haven, CT 06520

ROBERT C. STITES
President
Johnson & Johnson Baby Products Company
220 Centennial Avenue
Piscataway, NJ 08854

BRIAN SUTTON-SMITH, Ph.D.
Professor, Department of Folklore and Folklife and
Department of Education
University of Pennsylvania
Graduate School of Education/C1
3700 Walnut Street
Philadelphia, PA 19104

ROBERT B. ROCK, JR., M.A.
Director, Professional Relations
Johnson & Johnson Baby Products Company
501 George Street
New Brunswick, NJ 08903

HILDY ROSS, Ph.D.
Associate Professor, Department of Psychology
University of Waterloo
Waterloo, Ontario, Canada

PREFACE

This publication summarizes the third in the series of Pediatric Round Tables sponsored by the Johnson & Johnson Baby Products Company. In sponsoring this series the company has sought to provide support for a scholarly undertaking which will bring to interested parents and child health-care professionals new concept information at the leading edge of child development. The summary publication was written by psychologist-writer Paul Chance, Ph.D., and reviewed and edited by the other participating professionals.

The Round Table on play and learning covered six topics: 1) Interaction with Infants and Toddlers in the First Two Years, 2) The Growth of Pretending, 3) Exploration and Object Relations, 4) Play and Games at Later Ages, 5) Theory, 6) Overview of the Round Table. Material covered considers play from the point of view of theory: What is play behavior and what do we know about it? From the aspect of function: How does play contribute to infant and child development? From the vantage of application: How can we improve the quality of play experiences of children? In bringing together a group of internationally recognized scientists and child development professionals, the Round Table sought to address these questions and offer the best informed opinion about them. In summarizing their opinions in this volume, the Johnson & Johnson Baby Products Company seeks to offer parents and practitioners in the medical and caretaking fields a most sensible body of information on the subject of play and learning.

Robert B. Rock, Jr., M.A.
Director of Professional Relations

FOREWORD

Urie Bronfenbrenner, Ph.D.
Professor
Human Development and Family Studies
Cornell University
Ithaca, New York

For a culture built, as ours is, on the Protestant ethic of work and achievement, play presents a problem. As reflected in the forthcoming pages, it poses no less a problem for the scientists in our society than for its laymen. We have a difficult time defining play in positive terms, or according it a prominent place in our theories of human behavior and development, not to mention in public policy or practice. At the very most, play for modern man is an avocation, something that mainly children, and sometimes adults, do in their "spare time."

Given this orientation in our society and in our science, the words that follow take on an unorthodox cast, for I shall contend that play as a process lies at the very core of human behavior and development. It is the definitive text, whereas most of the rest is gloss written by particular societies and subcultures that are ephemeral from the perspective of history. Thus in the Western world, and in the United States in particular, the criteria we judge each other by when we are being most deliberate and objective—that is, by learning in the laboratory or in the home, by performance in school, on the job, or in the psychologist's testing room—these, I submit, are transient cultural epiphenomena; where we reveal our distinctive capacities and character most clearly—be it as individuals or groups—is in our play, what there is of it.

For evidence in support of this unconventional thesis, I shall not venture far. Most of it is contained in the pages that follow. In a world in which few people view play as a subject deserving serious study, the Johnson and Johnson Round Table has brought together most of those who do. They bring us rare resources. For, most of what is known about play in our times, they know—not only through scholarship, but through direct experience in the world of human play. They have shared the existing facts, insights, and interpretations with each other, and, in the pages that follow, Paul Chance has summarized this knowledge and thought for the rest of us in elegant and eloquent fashion.

Hence to set forth and support my thesis, I have only to highlight some of the themes my colleagues have sounded, and alert you, the listener once removed, to the contrapuntal and essentially harmonious pattern that I discern in the composition as a whole.

To begin with, play emerges in these pages as an *intrinsic* activity; that is, one that is done for its own sake rather than as a means to an end. Second, it is essentially *spontaneous* and *voluntary*, undertaken by choice rather than by compulsion. Third, play involves *enjoyment*; something that is done for fun.

So far, we have been dealing with universals—the distinctive properties of play in all its manifestations across a narrow, essentially mammalian phylogenetic spectrum. Be it a kitten playing with a bug, a bearded man with a balloon, puppies in a mock fight, children on a see-saw, dancers doing the "scuba scoop," or a couple absorbed in a chess game, the essential pattern is there: spontaneous activity for its own sake, with an element of *joie de vivre*.

But there are also other features of play that, while not definitive, are so often salient as to appear to have a special significance in their power to evoke the phenomenon. The first of these, illustrated in all of the above examples, is an environment that permits movement. A second, is the availability of movable objects. Third, it helps if these objects are alive, and, especially, if they are members of the same species. Finally, there is an additional qualification on the last point, evident in many of the examples cited by the Round Table participants, but not explicitly emphasized: fellow players are most likely to be parents and offspring, actual or potential sexual partners, or litter and age mates.

With these properties of play before us, I can now take my first step in moving from fact to inference in developing the stated thesis regarding the functional primacy of play in behavior and development; namely play is closely linked to the biological forces that impel, direct, and delimit action and growth. Accordingly, the fact that play is engaged in spontaneously, appears to bring intrinsic satisfaction, and is evoked by particular physical and social arrangements recommends it as a manifestation of the distinctive properties of the members of the given species as they respond to their environment at a particular stage in their ontogenic development.

The properties are distinctive at three levels. First, to the extent that play through the life course of a given species exhibits certain patterns that are invariant across settings in which the species lives, such patterns constitute evidence of species-specific characteristics in ways of responding to the environment. Second, to the extent that changing patterns of play throughout the life span are common to a particular group within the species, but not beyond, we can infer the existence of cultures or subcultures within the species. Third, to the degree that there are individual differences in play exhibited by members of the species living in the same setting, we obtain data on the dimensions along which organisms of a given species can vary their make-up and development level.

Here, then is a view of the scientific importance of play that argues for three kinds of empirical investigation. The first has to do with differences in forms of play exhibited by different species, something of a new dimension for comparative animal psychology. Of particular significance in this regard are the distinctive forms of play exhibited by Homo sapiens. The material presented by our circle of experts is instructive in this regard, for if we examine their examples we note that, in contrast to play in animals including nonhuman primates, much of our play exhibits a unique feature. *We bring elements into the situation that were not there before the play began.* Some of these elements are physical objects—toys, games, equipment. Others are non-tangible, but just as resistant; they take the form of rules about how the play is to be conducted. These are based on preexisting conventions and consensuses established in the society.

But the richest contributions a human player can bring to the situation are idiosyncratic; they consist of the products of his mind. The existing space and its content are elaborated in part through physical construction, but, even more, through being endowed with new meaning and transformed by the human imagination. Thus, boxes, blocks, and articles of furniture become houses, palaces, or entire kingdoms; doll figures, or mere pieces of wood, turn into mothers, children, fathers, cowboys, monsters, or what you will. Moreover, the imagined can become infinitely complex with family quarrels, comings and goings to school and work, messages sent here and there, great building enterprises and catastrophes—whole cities and empires erected and destroyed. Here, in Piaget's language, is the "child's construction of the world," and if we but take the time to examine it, I suggest we can learn much more about cognitive, emotional, and social development than whole batteries of intelligence tests, projective techniques, or psychiatric evaluations can tell us.

Some may say, this is exactly what psychologists and others have been doing—looking at play as a projective technique to tell us what is going on in the child's mind. Here I take partial but strong exception to a view of play widely held by many researchers and practitioners, but significantly, not even mentioned by our experts on the subject. Child psychologists and others have indeed been looking at play for many years, but, in my judgment, we have not been seeing much of what is there. And the reason is that we have lacked an adequate theory to enable us to recognize and describe the world of the child's construction, or, for that matter, of the adult's. The theories we now have, be they about children or grown-ups, all deal with *processes* taking place *inside the person.* For the experimental psychologists, these are the classical processes of perception, cognition, motivation, and learning; for the clinician, they are the psychodynamics of repression, conflict, and defense. Both kinds of operations can of course be analyzed in terms of their structure and development, but, and herein lies the missed opportunity, they are not the world that a child—or any developing person—experiences or creates. That world is perceived by the child, or any other "player," as existing *outside himself,* and that is the way we need to view it as well, as an external reality, a central aspect of the *environment,* its structure, its content, and the processes that occur in this externally organized context.

And that is where we students of human behavior are ill-prepared. We have developed elaborate and workable schemes for analyzing the human mind but not for describing the environments that the mind creates. At least not yet. But there is reason for hope, and it is found in the pages that follow. What is most impressive about the Round Table discussion is the evidence it provides of first steps in the development of conceptual frameworks for the systematic analysis of play viewed simultaneously in a biological and social context. It is precisely this task that must be pursued if we are to profit from what human play can teach us about the basic nature of human beings, as members of a biological species, as products of distinctive cultures, and as unique individuals. We owe a debt to the participants in the Johnson and Johnson Round Table for leading the way in this constructive course.

Chapter I

WHAT IS PLAY?

Play is like love: everybody knows what it is but nobody can define it. The difficulty of coming to grips with this deceptively simple concept, play, became apparent as Dr. Brian Sutton-Smith called the Johnson & Johnson Round Table on Play and Learning to order and the assembled experts wrestled with the question, "What is this thing called play?"

"I don't really know what play is," admitted Dr. Michael Lewis early on, "and it seems to me we're going to be hard put to arrive at an answer to that question." Dr. Howard Gardner agreed. Play, he said, is too complicated to be defined. Dr. Greta Fein argued that psychologists just don't know enough about play to come up with a clear-cut definition that everyone can accept. Dr. Robert McCall said flatly that defining play isn't important. After all, he noted, psychologists can't define intelligence, but that hasn't kept them from studying it. But definitions are central to science, and even those participants who despaired of arriving at a definition of play returned to the issue again and again. To understand the nature of a phenomenon means, essentially, being able to say what it *is*.

It turns out that it is much easier to say what play *isn't*. Dr. Jerome Singer, for example, suggested that play is what children do when they are *not* involved in activities that meet biological needs or that are required by adults. In other words, play is what children do when they are not eating, sleeping, going to the bathroom, or doing what their parents tell them to do. Similarly, everyone agrees that play is not work. As Dr. Corinne Hutt observed, tennis is play for the amateur, but work for the professional. Play is also not a game, though it's obvious that games are a form of play. The babbling of a baby in its crib, a jester making a pun, a college student getting stoned on pot—all of these activities can be and have been considered examples of play, but they are not games.

Finally, as Dr. Richard Chase observed, play is not a specific behavior, since a given act may be play at one time and not another. As Dr. Roberta Collard pointed out, if a child who can't swim falls into a swimming pool and makes flailing motions, that's not play; but if he makes the same motions while taking a bath, that is play. Dr. Barbara Kirschenblatt-Gimblett showed how culture affects which activities are considered play. To most Americans, she pointed out, lacrosse is a game, but to the Cherokee Indians, lacrosse is a religious ritual. And within a culture, what is play varies with age. A five-year-old child may sit on the living room floor in his pajamas and pretend he's driving a race car, shifting gears, roaring around hairpin turns, occasionally crashing into a retaining wall or another car and otherwise having a delightful time. But if an adult, or even an adolescent, does exactly the same thing, it is no longer play, it's schizophrenia. "It is just not possible," said Dr. Kirschenblatt-Gimblett, "to say this is play and only play and nothing but play."

One way of getting a handle on the concept of play is to identify the kinds of play, to come up with a taxonomy of play like the system of classifying animals that allows us to say that a giraffe is a mammal and not a reptile. There are, of course, lots of ways one could go about classifying play. A simple-to-complex format might start with the babbling of infants and end with a chess game. An evolutionary approach might describe the kinds of play found at each step on the evolutionary ladder, which range, according to Dr. Hutt, "from the frolics and gambols of young animals to the fantasies and intricate problem solving of man."

Or we might restrict ourselves to the human species and lump the kinds of play commonly found at each age level. Consider, for example, how play changes over the life cycle: babies play peek-a-boo and tickle-tickle; youngsters play cowboys and Indians and blind-man's bluff; older children play three flies in and spin the bottle; adults play golf and the stock market.

Then there are a number of play dichotomies: play can be social or asocial, cooperative or competitive, imitative or original, repetitive or novel, overt or covert, active or passive, organized or spontaneous, peaceful or boisterous.

One scheme that most experts find acceptable, if not ideal, identifies four kinds of play: physical play, manipulative play, symbolic play, and games.

Types of Play

PHYSICAL PLAY In physical or sensorimotor play the emphasis is on action. Young animals and young people both love to run, rough-house, and jump about. Young chimpanzees gallop, somersault, piroutte, and leap into the air, while rhesus monkeys drop thirty feet into the water over and over again. Most young primates, including children, spend a good deal of their time tickling each other, wrestling, playing tag, ring-around-the-rosy, hide and seek, king of the mountain, tug-of-war. The eminent Swiss psychologist, Jean Piaget, talked about "practice play," which included running, jumping, skipping, vaulting, hopping, cycling, and similar antics. Much physical play is, by its nature, social, boisterous, competitive. But what really sets this kind of play off from other kinds, in animals or children, is the amount of physical activity involved.

MANIPULATIVE PLAY   Some kinds of play are little more than attempts to manipulate, to get connrol over, or master the environment. "As soon as infants are able to reach out and grasp," said Dr. Hutt, "manipulative play is much in evidence." In part, manipulative play is a way of providing stimulation, as when an infant bats at the mobile that hangs over his head, or when a four-year-old girl, told not to handle the crockery on a table, complains that her arm will get bored if she stops! The sheer fun in figuring things out can also be seen in children who spend hours working jigsaw puzzles, fiddling with broken toys or taking apart their Mickey Mouse watches. Children get a kick out of making things happen, and every parent knows how manipulative children can be with people as well as with objects.

Dr. Gardner cited the example of a child at the kitchen table while his mother, her back turned, prepares dinner. "Cup, Mommy, cup," says the child. The mother answers without turning, "Yes, that's a cup." The child repeats, "Cup, Mommy, cup," and continues chanting the phrase until Mommy turns around, faces the child and says, "Yes, that's a cup." The child is not playing "What is this?" but rather, "Make Mommy turn around!" Much of play, then, is aimed at social control. The child is asking, Dr. Gardner says, "What will this person do? What happens when I do this?"

SYMBOLIC PLAY Symbolic play involves the manipulation, not of people or things, but of reality itself. Symbolic play includes what we ordinarily think of as pretend, make believe or fantasy play, but it also includes nonsense rhymes and other forms of speech play. In all its forms, symbolic play is, as Dr. Hutt put it, "quintessentially human." The antics of physical play are virtually identical for both children and monkeys, and the chief difference between a one year old chimpanzee and a one year old person engaged in manipulative play is that the chimpanzee is better at it. But one does not find monkeys or chimpanzees making up nonsense rhymes, building sand castles, galloping across the prairie on a broomstick or, cardboard sword in hand, rescuing a damsel in distress.

In a sense, pretend play is the deliberate misrepresentation of reality. "It involves," said Dr. Catherine Garvey, "some transformation of the here and now in which the child is actually situated." The settings, events, identities of objects or people, even attitudes and emotions can be altered for the sake of pretend play. The transformation can be made through language, the use of real objects, or through action. "The act of cooking," observed Dr. Gardner, "can be rendered linguistically, as when a child lists a number of ingredients; through movement, as when a child pours imaginary vegetables into an imaginary pot and stirs with an imaginary spoon; or through the use of objects, as when a child re-enacts a family Christmas dinner through the use of puppets, toy utensils, and other props."

Dr. Garvey identified three elements in pretend play: one

or more objects, a theme or plan, and roles. Any one or all of these elements may be fabricated or distorted to suit the player. For instance, a child can pretend to drink tea from a real cup, or use a sea shell as a pretend cup, or drink from a cup made out of thin air. The theme, plan, or story line in pretend play may reflect what goes on around the child, as in playing house, school, or doctor, or it may be a theme taken from a book, movie, or TV show, as when children play monsters or cowboys and Indians. The roles may also come from reality ("You be Daddy this time") or from the world of fiction ("I want to be Tonto; you were Tonto last time!")

Whatever transformation takes place, the child has complete control over reality:

"I stealed your cake."

"I don't care—it's not cake anymore."

He cannot be beaten:

"Hey, I shot you; you're dead."

"I'm not dead, I'm only wounded."

And if one fantasy is not to his liking, he may choose another:

"Pretend there's a monster coming, OK?"

"No, let's don't pretend that."

"OK. Why?"

" 'Cause it's too scary, that's why."

Pretend play may appear in very primitive form as early as eighteen months and possibly earlier, and is found in most healthy children by the age of three. It increases steadily with age into middle childhood and then begins to disappear; children seldom engage in pretend play after puberty. Instead, they daydream—which is really just a kind of internal pretend play.

Whatever form symbolic play takes, it is characterized by a lack of constraints. There are no rules that say you *have* to pretend in just this way, or that the theme of make believe must be plausible or even possible, or that speech play has to conform to the ordinary rules of grammar and syntax. This is not to say, however, that there is no logic at all to symbolic play. As Dr. Singer pointed out, if two little girls decide to play Mommy and Baby, and "Mommy" says, "Let's go for a ride," it will be Mommy who drives the imaginary car, not Baby. But the logic is to be found within the play itself, not in external reality. Dr. Kirschenblatt-Gimblett, whose special interest is speech play, observed that symbolic play has "a system of its own and is untranslatable, so that you have to deal with it within its own frame of reference, you can't translate it by referring to something outside of it." Most adults do not enjoy elephant jokes, nonsense rhymes and other forms of language play that children like because the adult's construction of reality is very different from that of the child.

GAMES When play is governed by rules or conventions, it is called a game. According to Piaget, very young children do not really play *with* each other; they may play side by side, but they do not interact in gamelike fashion. By the age of seven or eight, there is some cooperative interaction, but the rules that regulate their behavior are still vague. Not until puberty, says Piaget, do true games with clearly defined rules appear. But Dr. Hutt cited the research of R. R. Eifermann, whose 150 observers studied several thousand children of all ages and all socioeconomic groups in Israel. Eifermann found that rule-governed games started early and *increased* to age ten, then declined.

Dr. Dale Hay gave additional evidence that games appear earlier than Piaget thought. Dr. Hay described three studies of infants and toddlers who interacted with a parent, another child or an unfamiliar adult. Dr. Hay and her colleague found a number of interactions that they felt could only be called games. For example, Kathy, age one and a half, put a toy block in her mouth and her mother pulled it away saying, "Get that out of your mouth. Dirty." Two-year-old Tasha, who had been watching, picked up a block, put it in her mouth and walked toward Kathy. Kathy pulled the block out of Tasha's mouth and held on to it. Tasha went off and got another block, put it in her mouth, and came back to Kathy, who once again took the block from Tasha, and so it went.

Dr. Kirschenblatt-Gimblett objected to calling such interactions games, and suggested that they might better be considered "routines." Perhaps one reason for the uneasiness of some round-table participants on this point was the fact that these interactions often lasted only a few seconds, while games are usually thought of as more stable. But Dr. Hay argued that there is more to these interactions than is reflected in the word routines, a term that, as Dr. Hay said, "doesn't quite capture the playful quality we see in these interactions." And as Dr. Hay pointed out, the interactions that they came to call games had several characteristics in common that seemed very gamelike.

For one thing, there was mutual involvement. Whether the games were between two children, a child and a parent, or a child and a stranger, both people were actively involved in some *shared* activity. For example, if a child rolls a ball along the floor toward another child, who ignores the gesture and continues making mud pies, that is not a game. But if the second child responds by rolling the ball back to the first child, then the interaction begins to look like a game.

Secondly, the interactions were characterized by alternating turns. One child might throw a block into a tub, and then wait for another child to remove it. Often there were "turn signals," ways of saying, "I've finished; it's your turn." One infant, for example, stood by a tub, shaking it as he waited for an adult to drop a block into it. Another infant waved his hands impatiently at his mother in an apparent attempt to encourage her to return a ball.

Thirdly, there were repetitions of the entire interaction. In other words, there was a succession of turns, though sometimes there were only a few repetitions and there was no telling how long a game would go on.

Finally, there was a quality about the interactions that Dr. Garvey has referred to as "non-literality." That is, the activities of the game meant something more than their obvious literal meaning. If, for example, a child rolls a ball to someone and then walks away, that is a literal act: the child intends to give the ball away. But if the child rolls a ball to someone and then stands there facing him, smiling and holding out his hands, it is clear that he does not intend to give the ball away, but wants the other person to roll it back. He wants to use the ball as a way of having an interaction with the other person.

This classification of play into physical play, manipulative play, symbolic play, and games seems quite logical. Unfortunately, the distinctions implied are more arbitrary than real. Still, some sort of taxonomy seems essential, if only because it helps us see the range of activities that come under the heading of play. But taxonomies point out the differences better than similarities. In fact, after examining the myriad types of play, one might easily despair of ever reaching any agreement about what play is. Dr. Hay voiced this concern in a more narrow sense when she asked whether the activities she had called games in her research were really the sort of activity other people refer to as games. "How do our infant games relate to chess, hockey, hopscotch, or the Olympic Games? What is the commonality with tennis, Monopoly, or a simple game of catch?" The answer, Dr. Hay suggested, may be that there isn't any commonality, and she cited the philosopher Ludwig Wittgenstein to back her up:

> Consider for example the proceedings that we call "games" . . . What is common to them all?—Don't say, "There *must* be something common, or they would not be called 'games' " but *look and see* whether there is anything common to all . . . . Are they all "amusing"? Compare chess with noughts and crosses. Or is there always winning and losing, or competition between players? Think of patience . . . . Look at the parts played by skill and luck; and at the difference between skill in chess and skill in tennis . . . .

Wittgenstein's conclusion is that there is no single characteristic that is common to all games, which means there is no single characterisitic that is common to all kinds of play. The solution to the problem is not to look for a single trait, the *sine qua non* of play, but to look for overlapping characteristics, traits that run across many kinds of play, the way the fibers that make up a thread overlap. "And the strength of the thread does not reside in the fact that some one fiber runs through its whole length," wrote Wittgenstein, "but in the overlapping of many fibers." What fibers overlap in the thread of play? It would not be fair to suggest that the round-table participants reached consensus about this, but there did seem to be general agreement that at least five characterisitics are common to many kinds of play.

Characteristics of Play

PLAY IS FUN "The most distinctive feature of play," argued Dr. Hutt, "is its antic quality." Drs. Jerome and Dorothy Singer reported that they had collected data on measures of enjoyment in children engaged in fantasy play and have found that there is a definite correlation between smiling, laughing, and lively activity and involvment in fantasy play. "It's hard to tease out which is cause and which is effect," said Dr. Dorothy Singer, "but we see the two together pretty consistently." In other words, it's not clear whether children are happy because they are pretending, or whether they pretend because they're happy, but it either case, it's plain that when children play, they enjoy what they're doing.

The researcher who was most intent on the experiential aspects of play was Dr. Milhaly Csikszentmihalyi (cheek-cent-me-hi-ee). Play, he argued, has been too often thought of as something a person *does*, rather than something a person *feels*. "It is *playfulness* that concerns me," he said, "not play itself." Dr. Csikszentmihalyi has conducted in-depth interviews with assemblyline workers, secretaries, teachers, surgeons and mathematicians, as well as with people who spend a good deal of their free time playing chess, climbing mountains, dancing or playing basketball. He finds that those who get the most enjoyment out of the activity, whether it is somethng ordinarily thought of as play or not, describe a kind of mental state that Dr. Csikszentmihalyi calls "flow."

Perhaps the chief characteristic of flow is that there is an extremely high degree of concentration. The preoccupation with the activity itself is so intense that the person is unaware of other events. Dr. Csikszentmihalyi described the case of a surgeon so intent on the operation he was performing that he was completely unaware that part of the ceiling in the operating room had actually fallen to the floor! During flow, a person loses awareness of himself and the fact that he is enjoying what he does. "You are not thinking about doing something," said Dr. Csikszentmihalyi, "you are *doing* it."

While there was general willingness among the participants to accept the idea that play is ordinarily pleasant, there was less agreement about the role of flow in play. Said Dr. Hay, "I would hate to have us make the assumption that play is flow."Dr. Kirschenblatt-Gimblett observed that not all play activities produce the flow experence. "I've played many a game that I've been absolutely bored to tears with," she said. Dr. Chase picked up on this point and raised an interesting, broader issue: Is it the case that there are some kinds of play that people do not enjoy, or is it that when we no longer enjoy an activity, it is no longer play? "If you acknowledge," said Dr. Kirschenblatt-Gimblett, "that flow can be experienced in a whole range of activities not ordinarily thought of as play, what then is left of the concept of play? The solution to this dilemma, suggested Dr. Kirschenblatt-Gimblett, is that "you have to be able to conceive of play without flow as unsuccessful play." Dr. Csikszentmihalyi admitted that play and flow are not equivalent terms. "When the two coincide," he said, "it's lucky, but they don't have to go together." There is, in other words, more to play than having a good time.

PLAY IS AN END IN AND OF ITSELF   Closely related to the idea that play is fun is the notion that in play the activity is done as an end in itself. As Dr. Kirschenblatt-Gimblett phrased it, "In play, the center of interest is the process rather than the outcome, so that the *way* of doing something becomes what gets done." The fun in play comes from the activity itself, not from what one gets for it. "The pleasure in play comes from performing the act itself," said Dr. Hutt, who drew upon psychologist Daniel Berlyne on this point: "The chief element common to an infant shaking a rattle, a girl holding a doll's tea party, an adolescent football player, and the aged rake at the roulette table," wrote Berlyne, "is that they are all under the sway of intrinsic motivation." Similarly, Dr. Michael Ellis noted that "a common theme running through the notion of play is that it is inner-directed; in some way the rewards come from within the individual."

This is not to say that there are never any extrinsic rewards for play. A parent may, for instance, praise a child for playing nicely, teammates may cheer a fine performance, and winning is usually more fun than losing. But these external rewards are not essential to the maintenance of play. In fact, rewards can even take the fun out of play. As Dr. Csikszentmihali pointed out, research has shown that when children are paid with a toy or other reward for doing something they ordinarily do as play, the activity loses its appeal; the extrinsic rewards seem to reduce the intrinsic value of the activity. In other words, extrinsic rewards can turn play into work.

Dr. Csikszentmihalyi's own research shows, incidentially, that it is also possible to turn work into play. In work, the activity is a means to an end—a paycheck, a grade, an approving smile. In play, the activity itself is the end. Work can become play, then, if it becomes both means *and* end, both intrinsically and extrinsically rewarding. That may be a rare feat, especially since applying extrinsic rewards to play seems to take the play out of it, but, says Dr. Csikszentmihalyi, it is at least no longer necessary to assume that work must be unpleasant.

PLAY IS MORE THAN IT SEEMS   One aspect of play that reveals the importance of process over results is its non-literality. In play, the activities are not to be taken at face value, for what they literally are, but as a medium for play. There is, for example, something absurd about people struggling to acquire paper money, little plastic hotels, and boardwalk property in a game of Monopoly. Obviously, these objects are not important in their own right, but because they make play possible. "Games and other forms of play," said Dr. Csikszentmihalyi, "are only the packages for providing the experience of playfulness."

Dr. Thomas Shultz noted that it is often necessary to distinguish between the literal meaning of an act and its play meaning with a signal. In tickling an infant, for example, the adult must communicate somehow that this activity is play, perhaps by smiling and laughing as he tickles the child. Similarly, the smile that accompanies the push or slap, the laugh that follows a teasing remark, the wink that comes with the insult, are all ways of saying, "I'm only playing." And when a baby girl rolls a ball to another person and then waits expectantly for its return, it is clear that she is not really trying to get rid of the ball; she is saying, "Let's play!" There is, then, more to play than meets the eye.

PLAY PROVIDES A CHALLENGE   Activities that are either too difficult or too easy seldom qualify as play. In order to be play, an activity must ordinarily be difficult enough to be interesting, but not so difficult that it is impossible. Often the challenge is clearly defined, as in Monopoly and other games; other times, as in pretend and physical play, the challenge is open-ended, as much up to the player as is the solution. Play is at its best when the challenge nearly matches the skill of the individual.

Dr. Csikszentmihalyi's work on flow relates directly to this point. In his studies he has found that people are most likely to experience flow when the activity is of medium difficulty when compared to the individual's skill. Thus the degree of playfulness, or flow, follows an inverted U curve:

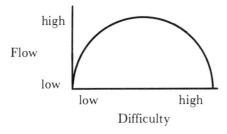

The grandmaster chess player would be bored to the point of nausea when competing against a novice, while the novice would probably be very nervous. Similarly, Dr. Csikszentmihalyi has found that new surgeons tend to get into flow during the simplest part of an operation, the closing, while more experienceed surgeons get into flow during the difficult stages.

It is partly this variability in skill that makes play so elusive, since what is impossible for one person is a snap for someone else: what is too difficult to be play for the two-year-old is too easy to be play for the six-year-old. Hence, the same activity can be play for one person and not another, play at one time and not another. Yet so long as a reasonable challenge exists, the activity is apt to be considered play.

Commented Dr. Ellis, "I play squash. Sometimes I feel pretty lousy about my performance, but it's the hope, the possiblity that tomorrow's game may go better, that next time I may get the shots I missed today, that brings me back to the court."

PLAY TAKES PLACE IN A RELAXED SETTING There is something about the social milieu in which play takes place that sets it apart from other activities. Dr. Hutt cited British psychologist Suzanne Millar's idea that "a certain degree of choice, lack of constraint from conventional ways of handling objects, materials and ideas is inherent in the concept of play." Said Dr. Chase, "In play a person is given a sort of diplomatic immunity from the serious activities of life." "Play," he added, "is something you have to get permission to do from a society that ordinarily stresses the important business of day-to-day survival."

Children are given the greatest amount of immunity from the usual expectations of society so they devote the greatest amount of time to play. The immunity is rescinded when we say to a child, for example, "Stop playing with your food." And as the child gets older, the permission to play becomes more and more restricted. Often in adults it is confined to very limited areas or times. "This is a big playground," Dr. Chase said of New Orleans (where the round table was held), "and there are lots of cues that say, in effect, 'we're not going to hold you to the usual expectations of society.'" Nightclubs, amusement parks, taverns, New Year's Eve parties are just some of the places where everyone understands that adults have permission to play. There are similar cues that tell children, "Now you are free to do as you please; now you may play."

These five elements of play do not run uniformly through all play activities. Rather, like the fibers in Wittgenstein's thread, they give strength to the concept of play only insofar as they overlap. They do not, therefore, provide a true definition of play. And, as some of the round-table participants said at the start of the conference, the search for a crisp, neat definition of play is probably futile. Definitions are always difficult in any field, and consensus among experts is a rarity. As Dr. Sutton-Smith pointed out, researchers focus on different kinds of play, so they inevitably come up with different definitions.

But the reason we try to answer basic questions such as "What is play?" is not because the effort will help us to identify the phenomenon better. As Dr. Fein observed, "Within a given culture, people know what play is and have little difficulty pointing it out." The value of wrestling with definitions is that it forces us to come to grips with a phenomenon, to throw away our simple, casual thoughts about it, to come to appreciate its subtleties, its intricate complexity. This is especially true with a concept like play, which *seems* so simple, so basic, so easy to understand. It is not.

Play is, like love, a complex phenomenon that deserves serious attention. It is a many-splendored thing.

Chapter II

WHAT GOOD IS PLAY?

Snakes do not play. Neither do crocodiles, earthworms or clams. In fact, across the broad spectrum of animal life, from the slimy to the sublime, those species that do play are a distinct minority. The great mystery, though, is not why so many animals don't play, but why some *do*. The infant snake pricks the wall of its leathery shell and slithers on its way. It plays no games, sings no songs, acts out no fantasies, and chases nothing it does not intend to eat. And it gets along just fine. So do the crocodiles, earthworms and clams.

Monkeys, otters, chimpanzees, and baboons, on the other hand, spend inordinate amounts of their time in play. So do children. One cannot help asking why. What possible value can such frivolous activities serve? To put it bluntly, what good is play?

Clichés assure us that play is a precious commodity: "Children learn through play," "Play is serious business," "The work of childhood is play." They assure us that play is essential to healthy development, that somehow play is useful to the individual and, ultimately, to society. But people have't always thought so. In medieval Europe there was no concept of childhood as we now conceive of it. There was a brief period of dependency, but as soon as the child was able to carry out chores, he did so.

Even today, one sees little play among children in subsistence societies, where nearly all the energy of the group is devoted to the serious business of staying alive. "You could see this clearly," said Dr. Sutton-Smith, "on the island of Mauritius in the Indian Ocean. The Mauritians eke out a bare existence, mostly by working on sugar plantations. One family I recall was typical: the father spent the day in the fields, cutting cane; the mother was with him, gathering leaves to feed the livestock; their children were at home, tending to themselves. I remember there was a girl about seven cooking rice on a ground-level wood stove outside the hut, a five-year-old held a baby on her lap, and a two-year-old sat on the ground nearby. There wasn't much play."

Throughout most of humanity's history, there hasn't been much play. Children were too busy gathering nuts and berries, tending fires, watching over infants, preparing meals. In the uncertain world of epidemics and famine, of marauding bandits and predatory animals, the margin for error was too small, the threat to survival too great, for the luxury of play. Everyone, even children, had to contribute to the survival of the group. Play would have been a useless, even dangerous, activity.

It is little wonder, then, that the first theories about play were little more than ways of apologizing for it. The nineteenth-century philosopher Herbert Spencer, for instance, noted that throughout history children had to generate huge amounts of energy to meet the exigencies of everyday existence. In modern societies the need for such energy no longer exists, said Spencer, and the result is a gigantic energy surplus. Play, then, is simply a means of using up excess energy.

The idea has a certain appeal to anyone who has ever wandered by a school playground just as the recess bell rang. "The children are like tiny particles of raw energy packed into a small container," said Dr. Ellis, "and when the're released, they explode into the open!" But the surplus energy theory is a rather cynical view of play which says, in essense, that the only value in play is that it tires children out.

Another theory of play came from the eminent American psychologist G. Stanley Hall. Writing just before the turn of the century, he argued that play was a kind of behavioral heirloom. It was "the motor habits and spirits of the past . . . persisting in the present." In other words, play was a reincarnation of ancient customs, beliefs, and skills long ago erased from conscious memory, but still visible in the freewheeling play of children. Like the tadpole that, in the course of its development, retraces the steps of its evolution, play reenacts the cultural evolution of humanity.

It is easy to find support for this theory too. All one need do is glance at any issue of *National Geographic* magazine and then watch children at play. The tribal ceremonies, the stalking of game, the shaman's magic—all seem to emerge in the spontaneous play of modern children. But once again, the assumption is that play is essentially useless. In this case, play has about the same status as the appendix.

It wasn't until this century that people began to think that play might have some value. Writing around the turn of the century, the Swiss scientist Karl Groos proposed that play was a way of preparing for adulthood. Children and many other young primates are incomplete; they have only the rudiments of the skills they need in adult life. Play is a way of exercising and refining those skills, a way for children to rehearse the roles they are destined to fill in adulthood.

This theory led to the notion that children might actually learn something from their antic activities, and play finally began to acquire a certain respectability. But the old negative feelings, what Dr. Sutton-Smith calls the "Scroogian ethic" of play, linger on. Our deep conviction that play is trivial reveals itself in comments such as "She's *only* playing," "Don't play with your food," "Stop playing around!" We can't help feeling that when children play they are doing something unimportant. We do not hesitate, for instance, to interrupt the boy and girl embroiled in a game of tug-of-war; but who would think of interrupting them unnecessarily while they are doing their homework? And much of children's play is so absurd, by adult standards, that it's difficult to find merit in it even when you look for it. When one ten-year-old asks another, "What do you get when you cross an elephant with peanut butter?" and the other answers, "An elephant that sticks to the roof of your mouth!" it's difficult to see just how such nonsense contributes anything to anybody.

Nevertheless, there is the growing conviction among many researchers and childcare specialists that play is not as frivolous as it looks, that somehow play does contribute to the development of the child and, ultimately, to society. Exactly what those contributions are and how they come about is less clear. Dr. Hutt, for example, raised doubts about the assumption that children actually learn *through* play. "We made a toy that had a number of switches on it," she said. "One switch made a bell ring, another made a buzzer sound, and so on. What we found was that the child would learn about these features when he examined the toy, but not when he played with it." If, for instance, a child learned about the bell during his exploration of the toy, and then began to play, the probability that he would learn about the buzzer was very low, unless he hit upon it accidentally. For Dr. Hutt, exploration, the intense examination of an object, an idea, or a skill, is where most learning takes place. Dr. McCall agreed, but felt that play provided a way of practicing what has been learned: "We often see children who suddenly acquire a new skill and then practice it over and over *ad nauseam* as if exercising it. Finally they master it entirely; they feel comfortable with it and they go on to something else."

"Yes," agreed Dr. Fein, "play is a place for exercising newly discovered skills, but it's more than that. Children don't just repeat what they've learned, they go beyond it. Play is a way of exploring that skill or that information further, of tapping its boundaries, finding its limits, mastering it." You see this, for instance, in fantasy play, when the role reversals lead to downright silly activity, and you see it in language play such as elephant jokes, where the children are testing the limits of meaning.

Whatever benefits play has may stem largely from the fact that play allows children to test the limits, to carry what they've learned as far as it will go. "Play," as Dr. Sutton-Smith asserts, gives us permission to make mistakes." The suspension of the ordinary standards, the playground atmosphere that Dr. Chase talked about, allows children to reach out, to trod unfamiliar ground. It is, as Dr. Csikszentmihalyi showed, those activities that match difficulty with skill that lead to flow, and it is just these kinds of activities that children prefer in play, activities that, as Dr. Sutton-Smith put it, "are not fully mastered, yet not completely unknown."

The freedom to fail, the permission to explore the impossible and the absurd, allow the child the opportunity to explore the outer limits of his skill, thereby gradually extending those limits. There is evidence, for instance, that children function at a higher level of sophistication in their play than at other times. Dr. Hutt reported on research comparing the language children used during play with their language at other times. "What one immediately notices," said Dr. Hutt, "is that when children play, their language is far more complex; not only are their utterances longer on the average, but they use more adjectives, more adverbs. On almost every measure, their language is far more complex during play than it is during their ordinary discourse." It is not just that children talk more during play, but that their language is more complex, more sophisticated. And it isn't just language that becomes more complex. Dr. Kirschenblatt-Gimblett described a study of four or five adolescents identified as problem children and slow learners. When the researcher, a graduate student under Dr. Kirschenblatt-Gimblett's supervision, studied their play, he was stunned. "They play street hockey on a busy street," said Dr. Kirschenblatt-Gimblett, "which means dismantling and removing the gear every time a car comes by. And the organization, the complexity of all the activities involved was vastly greater than those children seemed to be capable of in school. They were using skills that, in other settings, they simply did not seem to possess."

Dr. Kirschenblatt-Gimblett argued that there is probably a reciprocal relationship between play and learning. "Babbling and a lot of other linguistic play," she said, "precede language competence, but some degree of language competence is a prerequisite for more complex play. It isn't so much that you learn and then play," she went on, "as that there is some sort of reciprocity between play and learning." The idea is that there is a kind of play-competence spiral: learning leads to more sophisticated play, and play provides a kind of mastery that leads to more learning, which leads to more sophisticated play, and so forth.

In pretend play, for instance, the child creates a world of his or her own, but even though the child is its creator, it's a world that may teach the child things he or she did not know. Said Dr. Dorothy Singer, "The environment that the child attempts to create in a make-believe game is never quite what he expected it to be, and so in a sense the child finds himself in an unfamiliar place, a place full of interesting things to learn." That they do learn while in their fantasy world has been demonstrated, Dr. Singer noted, by a number of studies. For instance, research has shown that in the course of make-believe play, children learn a great deal about their surroundings.

Dr. Jerome Singer reasoned that children spend so much time in play that it almost has to contribute to their development in one way or another. "There is," he said, "a simply fantastic growth in a child's knowledge and skill during childhood, far beyond anything that occurs later on, and during this period the major activity of the child, at least in this society, is play. Children spend so much time in play, all kinds of play, that one can make a very good case for saying that the major learning experiences of people involve play." Whether learning actually takes place *during* play may be irrelevant. As Dr. Sutton-Smith observed, "It may not be that play is where things are first learned, but they are certainly nailed down in play."

One way or another, then, play contributes to the development of children in important ways. The play-competence spiral helps the child reach an adult level physically, intellectually, emotionally, and socially.

The Contributions of Play to Children's Development

PHYSICAL DEVELOPMENT The most obvious benefit from play is that it aids physical development. "Even the colonial Puritans," Dr. Sutton-Smith pointed out, "grudgingly admitted that vigorous exercise and sports contribute to good physical health," thereby providing for a long, productive life. Muscles and nerves develop with use and atrophy without it, and the physical exertion that comes with play improves circulation, aids in fighting obesity, helps maintain muscle tone, and increases resistance to a number of diseases.

But physical development also includes the acquisition of perceptual-motor skills. These skills depend a great deal upon experience, which means that they depend largely upon play. A child does not, for instance, simply pop out of the crib when his or her bones and muscles are sufficiently mature, and go for a walk. Walking means, among other things, keeping one's balance, and that requires learning to interpret and respond to the inner ear signals that say, "You're falling! You're falling!" Walking also means judging distances, estimating the slope of a grade, and coordinating what the eyes see with where the foot goes.

Grasping objects requires the same sort of perceptual-motor coordination. Three-month-old Charles, for instance, reaches for a small object with a large sweeping motion, palm outspread; at one year he reaches straight for the target and grasps it between index finger and thumb. Maturation has a lot to do with the improvement, but so does experience. The child's attempts to put a square block into a round hole are not so useless after all.

Perceptual-motor skills continue to develop throughout childhood, and play undoubtedly makes a contribution to that development. Building block towers and making mud pies; playing tug-of-war and pin the tail on the donkey; climbing trees and scampering through and around a jungle gym; playing space monsters and Tarzan; swimming, ice skating and playing baseball and tennis: all sorts of play involve the body's perceptual-motor equipment, and so aid in its development.

COGNITIVE DEVELOPMENT   The great American psychologist William James once wrote that the newborn infant enters a world of "blooming, buzzing confusion." But while the infant's ability to make sense out of the world is limited, he is not the empty-headed creature we have often assumed. "The old idea that the baby is a blank slate on which experience writes just doesn't hold up," said Dr. Lewis. In fact, research over the past two decades has shown that infants are not passive blobs of protoplasm that react only to the discomfort of a full diaper or an empty stomach. As one experimental psychologist has said, "Babies are bright for their age."

This does not mean, of course, that the infant emerges from the womb ready to study calculus. It takes time for mental skills to develop. "For example," said Dr. McCall, "at first objects to not exist 'out there'; they exist in the infant's body, in the sensations which they create." In other words, a smooth red rattle is only smoothness and redness and the sound of rattling. But by about seven or eight months, the baby begins to separate sensations from the objects that create them. He realizes that objects have existences of their own, that they do not dissolve into nothingness once they are out of view.

The child's grasp of language shows the same sort of methodical progression. Ask four-year-olds what an orange is, suggested Dr. Kirschenblatt-Gimblett, and they'll say, "You eat it." Give ten-year-olds the same problem and their answer is, "It's a fruit." To the younger child, a thing is what you do with it, but the older child realizes that objects fall into defining categories.

It is largely through play that this sort of progression takes place, for it is through play that children come to test the validity of their beliefs, to grapple with what they don't understand. Play is the trampoline on which the child springs to higher levels of thought. Dr. Shultz pointed out, for example, that babies do not immediately respond to tickling with giggles and smiles. "At first," he said, "they behave exactly as they might if they were under attack; they stiffen, they frown, they may even begin to cry. It is only with repeated experiences that the child begins to realize these are only *mock* attacks." With games like tickle-tickle and peek-a-boo, the child begins to grasp the concept of pretend, the notion that things are not always what they seem, that reality can be manipulated.

The ability to manipulate reality, to think metaphorically, is developed further through pretend play. Dr. Fein said that one of the chief benefits of this kind of play is that it allows the child to practice the art of making transformations, to explore the world of possibilities. It also gives the child the chance to try out his notions about the way the world works. Said Dr. Garvey, "What we see in play is not just wagons and soldiers, teacups and saucers, but the child's conception of the world, his grasp of morals, manners, sex roles, language."

Sometimes the child's efforts to make sense out of the world strike adults as amusing. Dr. Jerome Singer cited the example of a four-year-old playing on the floor with toy soldiers and cowboys. When he had lined them up in a neat row, he said, "We're going to rescue Daddy." His mother asked what he meant. "I heard you say on the phone that Daddy was tied up at the office," he explained.

Obviously, the child's first attempts to understand a concept may not be successful. But that's the beauty of play, since it gives the child the opportunity to try out new concepts, new ideas, new ways of thinking about the world— to try them out and, ultimately, to come to grips with them, to master them and then go on to some new challenge.

EMOTIONAL DEVELOPMENT When Sigmund Freud turned his attention to play, he concluded that it was often a way of coping with emotional conflicts. "Freud," said Dr. Collard, "believed that dreams have two functions, wish-fulfillment and mastery. When you think about it, play may serve the same functions as dreams. Much play is on the level of fantasy and also provides for wish-fulfillment and mastery."

Life among powerful adults is frought with frustrations and conflicts. The world is full of signs that say, "No Trespassing," "Do Not Enter," "Stop!" Children are too weak to rebel; they must accept reality as it is—except in play. In play, the rules are suspended. The child is no longer a weakling at the bottom of the hierarchy. In physical play, in games, and espcially in fantasy play, the child becomes master.

Whether play actually provides a kind of catharsis or not, there is evidence that play does contribute to emotional health. Children enjoy playing, and those who play more seem to be happier, even when they aren't playing, than those who don't play much. And those who are good at play, who are fun to play with, seem to get other emotional benefits besides the joy of play itself. Said Dr. Helen Schwartzman, "When you ask the children in a class who they like best, you find that the most popular kids are the ones who are the best at initiating and maintaining play." Thus, those children who play well also gain the good effects of having friends.

Children who have learned how to pretend are also able to escape unpleasant real life situations by withdrawing into a fantasy world that is much more entertaining. It is exactly this escaping from reality that gives some parents and child workers concern: all this pretend play, this creating fantasy worlds, isn't it bad for the child's mental health? Isn't the child likely to become a Walter Mitty, or worse, a schizophrenic?

Fortunately, the evidence points in just the opposite direction. Fantasy play seems to give children a clearer idea of what is real and what isn't. Perhaps, as Dr. Sutton-Smith argued, this is because the child is forced to recognize what things he can change and what things he cannot. "A lot of play," he asserted, "is an effort by the child to get power over his environment. But in pursuing this goal, he learns that some things cannot be altered." A child can, in other words, pick up a block of wood and say, "This is a dog," but the block of wood does not bark. Psychotherapist Karl Buhler, said Dr. Fein, once asked what a child would do if he were pretending that a stick was a doll and suddenly the stick talked. Would the child be surprised? "I've a feeling," said Dr. Fein, "that the child would be absolutely knocked out! Even though the child is bent on that stick being a doll, and having such and such personality and such and such a family, that doll is still just a stick—and sticks do *not* talk."

"A lot of parents ask me," said Dr. Sutton-Smith, "whether children who daydream, have imaginary playmates, and play make-believe games are in danger of becoming emotionally disturbed. I tell them that the main danger they're in is the danger of becoming a highly successful scientist or artist, because the research shows that these people engaged in a lot of play, including pretend play, when they were children."

Perhaps the single most important contribution of play to emotional development is the role it has in the formation of the child's self-concept. We learn about ourselves through our earliest interactions with our environment, espcially with the people around us. "The roots of our feelings of self-worth and competence," said Dr. Lewis, "are to be found in the cradle." And a great deal of those early interactions, even such pedestrian matters as feeding and diaper changing, involve play. Out of such apparently insignificant activities, the child begins to form hypotheses about the world and his or her ability to affect it.

By way of illustration, Dr. Lewis described two hypothetical babies, Sharon and Toby. Both are about the same age, both are healthy, normal infants. One morning Sharon is lying in her crib. She is wet or hungry and begins to cry. Nothing happens. She continues to cry, but nothing happens. After about five minutes of crying, she falls asleep, exhausted. On the same morning Toby, also wet or hungry, begins to cry. In a moment she is picked up by a friendly, attentive parent who changes her diaper or relieves her hunger. "Now," said Dr. Lewis, "what has happened? What have these two children learned about themselves and the worlds in which they live?" If this sort of pattern were to continue, Sharon would learn that the world is an unresponsive place, and that she has no way of altering her misery. She would become helpless. Toby, on the other hand, would develop feelings of competence, she would become a doer, a person who really believes that what happens to her in life depends upon what she does.

A number of studies offer support for this argument. When researchers compared institutionalized children with children reared at home, they found that the children did not differ particularly in what they were capable of doing, but they did differ in how much they used their abilities. Institutionalized babies, for instance, were just as capable of standing in their cribs, but they were far less likely to do so. The reason, Dr. Lewis argued, was that the institutionalized children got nothing for their efforts: nobody paid any attention. "They had learned to be helpless before they were six months old!" explained Dr. Lewis.

It is clear that play is one way in which the environment, including parents and other people, can respond to the child and contribute to his or her feelings of self-worth and competence. One of the reasons that this line of investigation is so important is that the feelings a child develops about himself or herself in the first few months seem likely to perpetuate themselves. Sharon's early failure makes her less likely to try to overcome future problems. What, after all, is the use of trying if trying produces the same results as doing nothing? Toby, on the other hand, is *more* likely to assert herself the next time she faces a problem.

Many of the opportunities that a child has to influence the environment come in play: the baby gurgles and a parent gurgles in return, the three-year-old throws a ball across the room and someone rolls it back, a six-year-old plays with a jigsaw puzzle and the pieces fit together, a nine-year-old tells a joke and others laugh, a twelve-year-old struggles with an Erector set and builds a bridge. Through such interactions, children acquire feelings about themselves that are vital to healthy emotional development.

SOCIAL DEVELOPMENT   Perhaps nothing is more characteristic of the human species than its sociability, a fact that long ago led Aristotle to call the human being "a social animal." Hermits exist, of course, but so atypical is their preference for isolation that we can't help thinking them somehow inadequate, perhaps mentally ill. Our sociability comes so easily to us that it seems automatic, as if we inherited our social skills the way we inherit the ability to sneeze.

Social skills do appear at incredibly tender ages. Research has shown, for example, that by the age of three months babies can recognize familiar people and are able to tell when their mother's voice is directed at them, and by twelve months they can identify a person's sex. These and other social skills develop so early and so effortlessly that we seldom think about teaching them. But they are learned, a fact that emerges clearly when something goes awry. "We had a girl in a day care center who had some serious learning problems," said Dr. Lewis. "One thing you noticed when you talked to her was that she did not look at you. She had not learned how to interact with people, how to direct her attention to them." Eye contact is an extremely important social skill, since it is the most basic way of making contact with another person, a way of saying, "We are together. We have a relationship."

The ability to make eye contact is just one of the social

skills acquired partly through play. Another is the ability to empathize, to be sensitive to the feelings of another person. One of the characteristics of pretend play is that it gives children the chance to take different roles, to experience the emotions of a fictitious character. Research has shown that children who engage in this kind of play are better able to tell what another person is feeling.

Pretend play also has the effect of giving the child a kind of *savoir-faire*, since it allows him or her to have certain experiences repeatedly even though in real life they are uncommon. "By playing 'doctor' or 'tea party,' for instance," said Dr. Dorothy Singer, "the child becomes familiar with the rules that govern behavior in those settings, and learns how to behave in those situations." That such practice can be useful is supported by the research of Israeli pyschologist Sara Smilansky, who demonstrated that children who played "school," later made an easier adjustment in kindergarten than did other children.

Children's games nearly always involve interactions with other people, so they are especially important to social development. The earliest games take the form of social rituals: the mother says, "Say, 'Momma,' " and the child responds "Ma-Ma." One of the things that children learn from such encounters is the concept of turn-taking. They learn, for example, that after they have taken their turn, they must pause to allow the other person to respond. This primitive notion of cooperation is elaborated into sharing and team work through complex games and through pretend play.

The opposite of cooperation is competition, and play is effective at teaching that concept too. Children learn about struggling toward an arbitrary goal, about rules, about aggression, about team spirit, and about the joy of winning and the misery of losing.

Play also helps children to understand all sorts of complex social concepts such as power relationships, hierarchies, social status, and roles. They acquire skill at the subtle art of communicating with people. Dr. Schwartzman gave this example: "When a child says, 'Let's play house' while facing a particular child, she is communicating her desire to interact with *that* child. At the same time, if she has her back to another child, the message she intends by *that* is equally clear."

The rejected child in this example not only learns about rejection, but about how to overcome it. "A child who is excluded from a game," observed Dr. Schwartzman, "might say, 'If I can play, I'll show you what's in my pocket.' " The ability to understand and use such tactics is an important part of social development.

The Contributions of Play to Society

It's clear, even from this brief analysis, that play does contribute more or less directly to the child's physical, cognitive, emotional, and social development. Play *is* useful, useful to the individual who plays. But what good is play to society?

There are a number of ways that society benefits from play. If, for example, play contributes to the physical and emotional health of children, society benefits too, since any society is better off if its members are sound and productive. And there is little doubt that having played in childhood helps adult members of society find ways of escaping the grind of modern life. All work and no play would make society a dull place. And, though it is difficult to gauge, it seems likely that the play of children provides a certain amount of comic relief, and keeps us from taking our own endeavors too seriously.

The most commonly cited benefit of play to society is that it is one of the chief ways by which children become enculturated. The stability of any group depends upon its ability to integrate new members into its fold. Small groups, such as fraternities, do this through an apprentice period. For society, the apprenticeship is childhood. The physical, cognitive, emotional, and social skills that a child develops through play are those that are useful in his or her *particular* culture. The amount of sophistication required to function smoothly in a given society is incredible, as any cultural anthropologist will attest: language, traditions, religious beliefs, morals, concepts about nature and property, hierarchies, and marriage customs; the list goes on and on. What comes only with intense, eye-glazing study to the anthropologist comes easily to people born and reared in that society. But people who are born in a society have a tremendous advantage over the anthropologist. For them, learning about their culture is, quite literally, child's play.

So one very important contribution that play makes is to integrate new members into the group, thus giving society stability. But modern, complex societies are not so much noted for stability as for change. They are not stagnant, they move. And play contributes to society by giving its members the ability to adapt to those changes.

"Play," said Dr. Sutton-Smith, "opens up thought. It generates a kind of flexibility or openness to new ideas, to new ways of doing things and new ways of looking at things." That flexibility, he argued, is what enables a society to change; it's what keeps innovations from becoming immediately and thoroughly rejected. It's what allows a society to move forward. For instance, over the past fifteen years our own society has seen drastic changes in the definitions of sex roles. There has been some resistance to these changes, but for most of us they have not been terribly hard to take. The shift is radical, yet our society shows little strain. Perhaps this is because the changes are not all that different from the sort of adjustments we learned to make in play. By taking hundreds of different roles and adapting to hundreds of rule changes in play, we have acquired a certain adaptability. We grope for a while as we struggle to understand the new rules, and then we go on as before. Younger people, those whose experience with such shifts in reality structure is most recent, have the easiest time adapting.

The movement of modern societies comes not only from the ability of its members to accept change; it also depends upon the ability of its members to produce change. "We always focus on the integrative function of play," said Dr. Sutton-Smith, "the way that play socializes children or brings them into society. That's what Piaget is after when he talks about assimilation through play. But play has an innovative function, too." At the same time that children are learning about the way society *is*, they are also learning to think about how it *might* be. That flexibility, that willingness to manipulate reality, Dr. Sutton-Smith believes, is what makes cultural change possible.

"What's really important about play," Dr. Schwartzman agreed, "is not that through it children learn the rules of society, or about specific roles or specific facts. What's important is that it teachers children that behavior has a context, and that the meaning of behavior depends upon its context." Truth is not, in other words, something etched indelibly on the wall of a cave, carved into a totem, or summarized in the *Encyclopaedia Britannica*. It is fluid. "That means," said Dr. Schwartzman, "that behavior and ideas can be commented on. They can be criticized, evaluated, revised, or rejected. This is what makes poetry, social commentary, art, science, and humor possible." Play, then, is the basis for cultural evolution.

That's speculation, of course. It's tough to prove that if a complex, modern society were to suddenly outlaw play its culture would stagnate or decline. Yet the idea is not entirely without support. The most gifted artists, scientists, and writers tend to have been particularly imaginative, playful children. And there is the fact that in societies that are moving culturally, play is different from that of more stagnant societies. "In primitive, authoritarian societies," said Dr. Sutton-Smith, "you find that much of the play is imitative; the kids play at what adults do. But in more advanced democratic societies, the play is often more varied, more imaginative, more innovative."

It's true, of course, that we could survive without play. Other species do. Their young do not spend hours chasing after one another, giggling, making up absurd jokes, jumping rope, or pretending to be the Lone Ranger, Big Bird, or an oak tree. *They* do not need play, and we could undoubtedly do without it, too.

We could also do without poetry, art, science, humor, and all the other things in our culture that make us so different from snakes, crocodiles, earthworms, and clams.

Chapter III

WHAT IS GOOD PLAY, AND WHAT WILL MAKE IT BETTER?

Even the teetotaler knows that some wines are better than others. So, for that matter, are some houses, some carpets, some cheese sandwiches. In fact, nearly everything can be rated from best to worst. So it is with play. It may be true that all play contributes to development, but it is certainly not true that all forms of play contribute to development equally.

It takes an expert to evaluate wines, to make the subtle distinction between a mediocre wine and one that is worth savoring. It takes a connoisseur to say, "This is good wine." Similarly, it takes an expert to evaluate play, to make the subtle distinction between play that does little more than occupy a child's time and play that makes an important contribution to development. It takes a connoisseur to say, "This is good play."

But how does one go about making such distinctions? What criteria can one use to evaluate the quality of play? How does a connoisseur go about answering the question, "What is good play?" The wine expert considers bouquet, color, body, and flavor. The round-table participants suggested four aspects of play by which it may be evaluated:

atmosphere, playthings, adult intervention, and individual differences.

Aspects of Play

ATMOSPHERE Atmosphere is a slippery concept. It's easy enough to say, for instance, that children will benefit most when they play in a relaxed atmosphere, but it's much more difficult to spell out exactly what a relaxed atmosphere *looks* like, or to say, in concrete terms, just what an adult can do to create one. It's clear, though, that atmosphere depends to a large degree upon the feelings supervising adults have about play. A number of conference participants pointed out, for example, that adults who adhere to the "Scroogian Ethic" are unlikely to provide a good play atmosphere. "People who think a child should be reciting the alphabet rather than singing ring-around-the-rosy," said Dr. Sutton-Smith, "are not going to encourage play."

It's hard to break loose from the feeling that play is frivolous, particularly in a society like ours, which puts tremendous emphasis on practical considerations such as economic success. We learn to be proud of what we know and what we can do, and a little ashamed of how much fun we've had. Many parents and teachers can't help feeling that time spent playing is time wasted. Children should sing songs, certainly—but why not a song that puts the names of the states to music? They should memorize rhymes, of course—but why not one that contains useful information, such as "Thirty days hath September . . . . ?" It's well and good for children to have fun, they believe, but it's important that the fun produce immediate, practical consequences, too.

It's necessary to emphasize that the opposition of adults to play is nearly always motivated by good intentions, not maliciousness. Dr. Hutt pointed out that people who distrust play have an implicit theory about learning that argues against play. "They believe," she said, "that learning results only from direct instructions: you learn when someone *teaches* you." There's always a hierarchy, with one person, the teacher, knowing more than another person, the student. "With this kind of theory about learning," added Dr. Hutt, "it's not surprising that play is viewed with suspicion."

Dr. Dorothy Singer told about the opposition she encountered when she tried to convince one group of parents that play was worthwhile. "We worked with nursery school children in a small town near New Haven, Connecticut," she said. "The parents of these children were mainly blue-collar workers, factory workers and the like, and they were very much against play. They were determined that their children would go further in life than they had, and they were convinced that play was their enemy. They wanted their children to spend their time learning letters, learning to count, accumulating facts. Then we came in and started trying to teach the kids to play. The parents weren't happy about that at all, yet these were good, sincere, honest people who wanted the best for their children. They just did not believe that play would help in reaching that goal."

But this antiplay attitude, however well-intentioned, keeps children from having many worthwhile experiences. Dr. Singer told about the good effects a positive atmosphere had on one child. "Sara never played," said Dr. Singer. "She was rated very low on imaginativeness and she usually sat in a corner by herself. She didn't interact much with the other children or even make use of the toys around her. For two weeks she sat near me and watched as I molded some clay, but she never got involved; she just stared at me with a sour look on her face. I thought that we weren't getting through to her at all, that we were making no impression. Then one day there was a good deal of excitement in one part of the room and I peeked around a corner to see what was going on. There was Sara sitting at a table with four other children and she was directing them in pretend play. She set the table with imaginary plates and forks, she served imaginary food, the whole works. She even reached under the table and fed an imaginary table scrap to an imaginary dog! It was just great, and she had the kids jumping with excitement. I've never seen a child play more imaginatively, yet a couple of weeks before this child showed almost no imagination or social skills at all." When Sara's mother saw the transformation play had brought about, she began to feel more positively about play.

Even adults who have a positive attitude toward play can provide a less than ideal atmosphere if they are too vigorous in setting up restrictions on a child's behavior. "People who believe that children should be seen and not heard," said Dr. Kirschenblatt-Gimblett, "that they should speak only when spoken to, are not likely to create an atmosphere that is conducive to play." Nobody at the conference suggested that a good play atmosphere required that a playroom had to match the noise level of Kennedy International, or that children had to be given the power of czars. A good play atmosphere does not, in other words, inlcude the right to tear down the house. On the other hand, it's difficult to imagine children playing well if they have to constantly monitor their behavior to make sure they are quiet, that they aren't getting their clothes wrinkled, or aren't breaking some other rule. There have to be limits, but there have to be limits on the limits.

In summary, the chief ingredient in a good play

atmosphere is freedom—freedom to move about, to touch things, to try things out, to experiment, to explore. But most important, the child needs freedom to make mistakes, to perform imperfectly. One thing that sets play off from other activities is that there are no evaluations, no grades, no scores, no real failures. In play, a person gets to do something and fall flat on his face without feeling bad about it. It is probably because of this freedom that children perform at more sophisticated levels during play than at other times. If they misuse a word, if they distort a concept, if they say something foolish, there's no penalty. Adults who constantly watch for mistakes, who sit in judgement on how the child plays, on how well he or she performs, will create an atmosphere that is about as conducive to good play as is a dental office.

Of course, the physical environment also affects the atmosphere. Dr. Chase suggested that an area that is bright and cheery and generally attractive is helpful. A play area can be painted in bright, happy, and playful colors, it can be striped or checkered or plaid or painted with murals. Or it can have sliding walls that will allow for frequent changes in decor to give the room additional novelty. The walls can have posters. The room can be furnished with "hands on" sculptures. And it goes without saying that the play area should be safe; alleys full of broken bottles and nails and other dangers that the child has to be alert for do not facilitate a carefree, playful mood. It will also improve things if the environment is designed with children in mind: playgrounds, for example, usually have jungle gyms and other equipment scaled for children of different shapes and sizes, but houses typically have giant-size (that is, adult-size) chairs, tables, dressers, and other furnishings.

One aspect of the physical environment that is important

is the degree to which it allows for privacy. Dr. Jerome Singer noted that there is some evidence that children who come from homes offering privacy are more imaginative in their play. In fact, the number of people per room turns out to be a fair indicator of the creativity of the children in that house; the more space available to each person, the more creative a child is apt to be. It's probably desirable for the child to have his or her own room, if possible. Another way to manufacture a little artificial privacy, either in the home or in the nursery or the school, is to set off a certain area as a privacy corner. Room dividers can help designate small islands which can be occupied by only one person at a time. This way a child who wants to go off by himself for a while can do so, although there may be some interruptions from meandering playmates.

So, to create an atmosphere that is favorable to play, adults must create a physical and psychological environment that gives children permission to play and encourages it when it occurs, an environment that says, "Play is OK. It's an acceptable thing to do, a *good* thing to do. Go ahead, enjoy! Enjoy!"

PLAYTHINGS Toys are an important part of a child's environment, and they can help to provide a good play atmosphere. But even the child who lacks a single commercially produced, Good Housekeeping Approved, genuine toy has playthings; the infant, for example, has the feet at the other end of the crib; the two year old has a saucepan and spoon; the young school-age child has hills to roll down, trees to climb; the older child has butterflies to collect and friends to wrestle with. Children are marvelously inventive, provided their inventiveness is not squelched by an overly restrictive atmosphere, and they can turn nearly any object into a plaything. But that doesn't mean that all playthings are equal. Just as one kind of atmosphere facilitates good play, while another kind of atmosphere discourages it, so certain playthings are more beneficial than others.

Obviously, playthings ought to be safe, although it's probably true that a perfectly child-safe object has never been built. Even unbreakable toys have been known to fragment into sharp edges once a child put his mind to it, and any object that is light enough to be thrown can be turned into a dangerous missile. But some objects are clearly more hazardous than others. Generally the features that make a toy dangerous are fairly obvious: it doesn't require a Ph.D. in engineering to know sharp edges can cut, that toys that propel darts through the air have the capacity to blind, and so on. Other hazards are less apparent: toys covered with lead-base paint, for example, can result in brain damage if a child amuses himself by chewing on them, and some toy stoves can produce dangerously high temperatures. The Consumer Products Safety Commission publishes lists of hazardous toys as well as safety guidelines that parents and child-care workers will find helpful.

Given that the playthings available to a child are carefully selected to exclude those that might do bodily harm, which ones will help the child get the most benefit from play? What qualities mark those playthings that facilitate good play? Playthings vary in the degree to which they are realistic. A wooden truck can be a faithful imitation of the real thing, right down to the license plate and the hood ornament, or it can be a highly stylized version that barely resembles the profile of a truck. Which truck is a better toy? The role of realism in playthings is something that Dr. Fein has taken some pains to understand. Her work inclines her to believe that very young children (under two years old) have a difficult time engaging in play with highly unrealistic toys. It's not that objects that don't look like what they represent are physically harder to play with. "The difficulty," Dr. Fein pointed out, "comes from the youngster's inability to make the transformation, to treat an oblong block of wood *as though* it were a truck." The more realistic a toy is, then, the easier it is for a child to use it as the object it represents. As the child gets older and acquires imagination, the object need not be so realistic. The physical attributes of an object that say, "This is a truck," are a kind of crutch that the young child needs for good play. Later, that crutch may only get in the way. An object that only vaguely resembles a truck can be used as a car, a tank, or perhaps even a shovel or a hammer, but a toy truck that really looks like a truck is hard to make into a hammer. So, it would seem that for very young children, highly realistic toys are more desirable, but as children get older, less realistic toys may get better results.

A dimension of toys that is similar to realism is their degree of structure. A structured toy is one that, by its very nature, implies certain limitations about the way it can be used. In other words, an unstructured toy requires more from the child, whereas a structured toy requires less. Clay, blocks, and finger paint, for instance, are unstructured toys, while trucks, dolls, and tea cups are highly structured ones. Dr. Fein cited research that showed that among five year olds, those who were highly imaginative and adept at pretend play preferred the unstructured toys; those who were less imaginative preferred the structured ones. And there is some evidence that when children play with unstructured toys, they produce far more imaginative stories. It seems plausible, then, that as children get older they will benefit most from less structured toys.

Another aspect of toys is their novelty. Dr. Collard described a series of experiments showing that even infants are attracted to the new and unusual. In one experiment, for example, she gave a series of similar objects to infants aged eight to twelve months and let them play with each of them for a brief period. After they had played with the objects, Dr. Collard offered the babies a choice of two new objects, one similar to the series of toys, the other different. She found that the infants were much more likely to select the novel item. This preference for the unfamiliar is handy, since we learn more from new objects than we do from old ones. To stimulate a child's interest in the world around him, to keep him actively exploring that world, it will help to provide novelty. Does that mean that adults should buy new toys every day? Not at all.

Some toys are inherently more novel than others. They have many sides, many colors, or they can change shape. Dr. Chase, who has spent several years developing toys that will stimulate as well as entertain children, has designed an infant toy he calls the Visual Display. The Visual Display has plastic walls covered with various figures and brightly colored designs. Each side of the Visual Display can be reversed to show a different design. So even though the Visual Display has a limited number of figures and designs, its various combinations give the toy considerable novelty.

Dr. McCall suggested that the same sort of novelty can be built into other toys. Parents often suspend a mobile over a baby's crib, but it rarely occurs to the parents to modify the mobile. Discs, balls and other objects on the mobile can be replaced from time to time. This can be done easily by hanging the mobile parts on string loops that slide on and off of the arms of the mobile.

Another way that toys can be given greater novelty is by mixing unrelated toys together. Dr. Shultz described research by one of his students on the effect of various combinations of toys on play. Some youngsters were given three toys that were logically related: a shovel, a rake, and a watering can. Others were given a more peculiar set of toys: a shovel, a boat, and a telephone. After playing with the toys, the children were asked to name as many uses as they could think of for a shovel. Those children who had played with the odd combination of toys gave more original answers than those who had had toys that went together. Thus, the odd assortment of toys that ordinarily accumulates in a play area may be more beneficial than an orderly collection of logically related toys.

One important aspect of a plaything is the degree to which it encourages the child's participation. Toys that "do it all" may be less desirable playthings than those that require the child to participate. This may be why less realistic, less structured toys lead to more imaginative play: they require inventiveness. A mobile, for example, can be suspended over a crib where the baby can view it passively, or it can be brought within reach so that the child can tap its various parts with a hand or foot. In the latter case, the toy is more responsive; the behavior of the child has an effect on it. Dr. McCall offered another example of a responsive toy: "Suspend a bar, as I did with our children, across the crib, and hang attractive objects from it. Then tie a brightly colored cotton yarn loosely around the baby's foot or wrist and tie the other end to the bar, so that when the baby moves, the bar and the objects move."

Dr. Lewis suggested that responsive toys teach a child that his or her behavior has consequences. When a child moves his hand and the mobile moves, there is a cause-and-effect relationship. At first the child's movements are accidental, and the movements of the mobile a coincidence. But gradually the child realizes, "Hey, *I* made that thing move." That sort of control over the environment, said Dr. Lewis, can be extremely important not only in teaching the child causal relationships, but in giving the child a sense of competence, a sense of power.

An issue closely related to the responsivity of toys is their complexity. In general, it seems that the more things a toy does, the less the child does. And the more passive a toy renders a child by doing things for him or her, the less desirable it is. Does this mean that the more complex a toy is, the less beneficial it is? Not necessarily. "It's not the complexity of the object itself that counts," said Dr. Ellis, "but the complexity of its uses." This "functional complexity" has little to do with the intricacy of an object. A television set is a highly complex item, but the interactions that it induces in the child are generally very simple. A rubber ball, an extremely simple object, has a good deal of functional complexity; it can be bounced, rolled, thrown, squeezed, hit with a bat, spun around, tossed in the air. And the child's use of the rubber ball almost certainly teaches him more about the laws of physics than he would learn from watching Superman leap over tall buildings in a single bound.

"The most functionally complex playthings," said Dr. Ellis, "are people." Nothing is more variable, more capable of multiple interactions, than a person. So toys that encourage interaction with other children are especially desirable. The rubber ball, for example, can be played with when the child is alone, but its uses multiply when it is used in play with another person: So, too, with the doll, the magic kit, toy trucks, empty cardboard cartons, and hundreds of other objects.

ADULT INTERVENTION The role of other people in play brings up the matter of adult intervention. There seemed to be consensus among the round-table participants that children have a natural predisposition toward play. That does not mean, however, that the adult's role ends with providing a suitable atmosphere and appropriate playthings. "While chillren show a certain amount of play spontaneously," said Dr. Jerome Singer, "it often drops off as time goes by unless there is some sort of active adult intervention." Dr. Hutt pointed out that some people assume that, since children learn through play, all one need do is allow children to play and they will automatically learn. "There could not be," she noted, "a more well-intentioned but misguided view." A child playing alone in a sandbox, for instance, will typically engage in rather stereotyped activities, scooping and pouring sand. The child no doubt acquires some information as well as some sophistication in eye-hand coordination from such activities, but after a time the benefits are minimal. "The intervention of an adult at such time seems imperative if play is to contribute to development," said Dr. Hutt.

The adults who supervise children are, then, an important element of good play. The question then becomes: How should adults intervene? There are a number of intervention strategies, but the most important principle seems to be that the adult should actually participate in play. "The adult needs to take part in play, not *talk about* it," Dr. Sutton-Smith said emphatically. Some adults are all too willing to intervene in play, but they want to do it by offering instructions. They are eager to tell a child what to do, to show him or her the "right" way of going about building a sand castle or throwing a ball. Instructions are not necessarily bad, but they run the risk of undermining the play atmosphere. The best tactic is to play *with* the child, not merely supervise or direct his play.

For some adults, that's a tall order. Drs. Jerome and Dorothy Singer noted that many parents and teachers feel very uncomfortable when playing with children. Directing a child's efforts in a game of jacks is one thing; playing jacks is quite another matter. The Singers noted that in their efforts to work with parents,they have had to try to rekindle the art of playfulness in adults so that they could play easily and naturally with their children.

Another way that adults influence the quality of play is by providing good play models. The best way to do this, again, is by the adult's active participation in play. In the case of Sara cited earlier, Dr. Dorothy Singer provided a model by working in clay. A number of studies have shown that children can learn to play by watching others play. The results are especially good when the adult model engages the child in the play activity. In one study by Drs. Jerome and Dorothy Singer, for instance, preschool children were led in pretend play by an adult for half an hour a day. After two weeks of this training, the children were more adept in their own pretend play. Children who had watched *Mr. Roger's Neighborhood* on TV in the company of an adult who interpreted what took place on the screen also benefited, but not as much as those who actually played with an adult. Simply watching the television program alone did not improve the quality of pretend play, but did keep the amount of spontaneous pretend play from dropping off.

In addition to participating in play with the child and modeling desirable forms of play, there are other, more subtle aspects of adult intervention that are important. Dr. Fein, for example, discussed the role of specific kinds of adult activities. Working with mothers and their eighteen- to twenty-four month-old infants, Dr. Fein coded the kinds of parental responses to children's play activities. She noticed that some mothers typically engaged in highly imitative acts: the child would bang on something with a spoon, and so would the mother; the child would gurgle, and so would the mother, and so on. Other mothers were more elaborative; that is, they would expand on what the child did by modifying it in some way: the child would bang with a spoon and the mother would bang with a stick, or the child would bang with a spoon and the mother would pretend to eat with the spoon. Other mothers would engage in unrelated or disconnected kinds of responses: the child would bang with the spoon and the mother would push a truck. The different kinds of interactions seemed to yield different results. "Kids whose mothers use a lot of elaborative play do very well on intelligence tests," said Dr. Fein, "while those whose mothers engage in disconnected responses don't do nearly as well." Those whose mothers are imitative fall between the other two.

Another important aspect of adult interaction is its responsivity. Just as toys can be responsive to the acts of a child, so too the adult's behavior can be responsive. In fact, it may be responsivity that underlies the finding of Dr. Fein that disconnected play is not as beneficial as are imitative and elaborative play. Disconnected activities are, by definition, unrelated to the behavior of the child. The child and adult are playing, but it is parallel play; they are not interacting with each other.

The difference is critical: if the adult *responds* to the actions of the child, the child's behavior has consequences. But if the adult's play is merely parallel to the child's, then the child's behavior has no effect. As Dr. Lewis pointed out, when a child's behavior produces consequences, it gives the child a feeling of competence.

The degree to which an adult interacts with a child in a responsive manner is more important than how often the adult and the child interact. Dr. Lewis cited a series of studies that show that the mental abilities of three-month-old infants are not related to the *number* of interactions of a mother with her child but such abilities are related to how responsive the mother is. In other words, the mental benefit an infant gains from interactions with his or her mother comes not so much from how *often* the mother smiles at, talks to, touches, or otherwise interacts with a child, but rather the degree to which those parental acts are in *response to* the behavior of the child.

In general, the researchers seemed to feel that the more an adult plays with and is responsive to a child, the better. Dr. Fein, for example, cited research showing that when very imaginative children were compared with less imaginative children, it was found that the former spent more time playing with their mothers. It is possible, of course, to get too much of a good thing, and adults need to know when to back off. Dr. Jerome Singer cited the work of psychologist Marc Gershawitz on this point. Gershawitz found that adults who initially showed a good deal of direction, but then gradually withdrew and left the children to their own resources, got the best results. Adults who keep this in mind should be able to strike a happy medium between ignoring a child's play and dominating it completely.

INDIVIDUAL DIFFERENCES Finally, good play depends upon the characteristics of the individual child. What is appropriate for a boy of two is inappropriate for a boy of four. There is also tremendous variation among different children of the same age. Even infants differ widely in temperament, in activity level, in the amount of curiosity they show, in physical and mental abilities. These differences do not shrink with age; they expand. We can be fairly certain that a one-year-old child—*any* one-year-old child—will get little benefit from a sophisticated language game such as Scrabble. But we can't be so confident that this sort of play will be wasted on an eight-year-old. Some eight-year-olds will have the language skills and temperamental qualities that would make Scrabble a good game for them, while many other eight-year-olds would get little fun or value from it.

Physical maturation provides a good example of the idiosyncratic nature of development. The average age at which children begin to walk is thirteen months. But some children begin walking at eleven months of age or younger, while others don't get around to it until they're fourteen months old or more. Mental development follows a similar pattern. Some children say their first words at ten months of age, while other perfectly normal children do not reach that stage until the twenty-fourth month. The research of Dr. Csikszentmihalyi showed the importance of taking the skill of a child into account. Flow—the fun in play—is not related to the difficulty of an activity, per se, but to the degree to which it matches the abilities of the child. The value of play, then, hinges partly on the extent to which it provides a challenge, but not an impossible challenge, to the child. That can only be gauged by watching the individual child; it cannot be derived from charts on the development of "typical" children.

There are other differences among children, and within the same child at different times, that help to make life interesting for those who work with children. These are not so much differences in ability as in style. Temperament, for example, varies a good deal among children. Some infants scream and holler at the slightest excuse, while others can't be provoked however much the world torments them. Some preschoolers have an inexhaustible supply of questions, while others simply stare inquisitively at a new phenomenon and then go about their business. Dr. Gardner discussed recent research on differences in "cognitive style." "In a typical experiment," he said, "we give children a bunch of blocks of different sizes and colors, and then we watch to see what they do with them. What we've noticed is that some children are fascinated by the way the blocks relate to one another. They'll lay them out in a row or build a tower or arrange them into some sort of Stonehengian structure. They seem to be preoccupied with the way the blocks are arranged, with their pattern, so we call these kids Patterners. Other kids take an entirely different approach; they'll pick up two blocks, one in each hand, and they'll say, 'This is the mommy and this is the baby and they're going to the store.' For these kinds, the objects are just props for telling a story, so we call these children Dramatists." It's not that one child is functioning at a higher level than the other, they just function differently. So far, the research suggests that in the second or third year of life, most children favor one style over the other. After this, they usually alternate from one style to the other as the situation demands. But even into the school years, roughly a third of the children seem to show a consistent preference for dramatizing or patterning. These differences in cognitive style may affect what an individual child considers play, as well as what benefit he derives from a particular play activity.

Sex differences can also influence what a child gets from play. Much to the chagrin of boys, girls develop faster, both in physical skills such as motor coordination and in mental skills such as language, until about age eleven. Then the trend reverses and girls tend to lag behind. The adult who is sensitive to such sex differences can, for example, forestall some of the sense of inadequacy a boy may feel in a family of two younger, but more competent, girls.

There is also some evidence of sex differences in the kind of playthings children prefer. Dr. Fein's work on realistic and unrealistic toys suggests that girls seem to benefit more from playing with unrealistic toys, while boys often get more from realistic ones. Whether these differences are somehow tied to biological differences, such as maturation, or to some cultural factor, is not clear.

The role of culture in the value of play was stressed by Dr. Chase. "Children differ," he said, "not only in things like ability, temperament and cognitive style, but in the groups to which they belong." Like adults, children come from different social backgrounds, they have different religions, different values, different languages. Some live in rich neighborhoods, with access to every sort of cultural advantage, while others live in poverty. The social milieu in which a child lives has a profound influence on the way he or she interacts with other children, with adults, even with objects. A nursery school teacher who hands an orange to a ghetto child may be surprised to find the child trying to bounce it like a ball. The teacher may be annoyed by this "mischief" until he or she realizes that fruits are less common in the home of a ghetto child than they are in middle-class homes. Where oranges are a rarity, they may be reasonably mistaken for balls.

So the value of play depends in part upon the characteristics of the individual child. This complicates life for adults, since children vary so widely and in so many ways. It is inconsiderate of children to be so variable, but it can't be helped.

It would be convenient, to say the least, if the round-table participants could have offered some sort of formula by which individual differences in physical and mental development, in cognitive style, in temperament, and in social background could be taken into account to tell the adult just what sort of play would be ideal for a given child at a given time. Better yet, why not a computer that would assess atmosphere, playthings, adult intervention and the individual characteristics of the child and then, after a suitable period of whirring and sputtering, crank out a list of simple instructions for providing the best play possible? Apparently there is as yet no computer smart enough to tackle the task. Computers are stuck at the level of such trifling matters as defeating chess masters, computing statistical analyses, and solving quadratic equations. They are not yet up to so difficult a problem as deciding what makes for good play.

That riddle is left to the parents, teachers and other adults who work with children. They must study the psychological and physical environments to determine whether they provide the best possible atmosphere; they must examine the playthings available to the child to see if they offer more than clanging bells and whistling sirens; they must assess their own interactions with the child and decide if their intervention facilitates or interferes with play; and they must get to know each individual child under their care, to know his or her idiosyncracies and how they affect what the child gets from play

It is, in other words, the parent, the teacher, and others who work with children who must do what the computer cannot. It is *they* who must become the connoisseurs of play.

Chapter IV

WHAT? MORE ON PLAY!?

The Round Table on Play and Learning brought together many of the leading authorities on play and its role in development. I attended the conference, studied the transcript of the proceedings, and read a number of technical reports published by the participants. Then I tried to synthesize that material into a kind of nutshell summary of what the experts have to offer parents, teachers, nurses, day care workers, pediatricians, and others who work with children. But this booklet is only a beginning. You may want to follow up on this introduction by reading other treatments of the topic. A number of readable and informative publications are available.

Brian and Shirley Sutton-Smith have written a book called *How to Play with Your Children — and When Not To* (Hawthorn Books, 1974; $3.95 in soft cover). This book, intended primarily for parents, follows a chronological progression from birth to adolescence. It covers topics such as mastery, the importance of pretending, and dreams.

The Johnson & Johnson Baby Products Company has put together a package that will be of special interest to parents of children one year old and younger. It includes thoroughly researched toys, including the Visual Display mentioned earlier, and a well-illustrated book covering social and emotional development, physical development, and play and learning. The package is called the *Infant Development Program* and it's available from Johnson & Johnson (1977; $49.95).

Dorothy and Jerome Singer have recently coauthored a book called *Partners in Play* (Harper and Row, 1977; $10.95). The book is a step-by-step guide to helping children develop imaginative play. Its chapter titles include, for example, "Magical Changes: Learning About Ourselves and Others Through Play," and "Using Television Constructively for Imaginative Growth."

The Educational Testing Service in Princeton, New Jersey, publishes short, readable booklets on the work of their researchers. One booklet, though very brief, is relevant to our topic. It describes recent findings on mother-child interactions and the effects of different kinds of interactions on child development. Much of this work was done by Dr. Michael Lewis. The booklet is called "The Cradle of Behavior" and is available from ETS at no charge. Write to Information Division, Department CB, Educational Testing Service, Princeton, New Jersey 08540.

There are also interesting sources about toys and other playthings. The Toy Manufacturers' Association publishes a free booklet on toy safety. Write to Ted Erickson, 200 Fifth Avenue, New York, New York 10010. For those who are looking for free or inexpensive playthings, a subscription to *Freebies* may be worthwhile. This is a monthly magazine that provides information on items you can get free from publishers, pharmaceutical companies, government agencies, and so on, simply by requesting them. Often the items include toys, posters, games, and the like. A one-year subscription is available for $5.00 from *Freebies*, P.O. Box 5605, Santa Monica, California 90405.

If you get really serious about play, you might want to look into some of the more scholarly sources on the subject. Dr. Schwartzman, for instance, has just written a book on the anthropology of play called *Transformations: The Anthropology of Children's Play* (Plenum, in press). This book is well worth the attention of people who work with children from non-Western cultures. Dr. Garvey's new book, *Play* (Harvard University Press, 1977; $6.95); offers, among other things, a detailed discussion of the kinds of play. Dr. Garvey's and Schwartzman's books are heavier reading than the other sources mentioned here, but they can be read profitably even by those who lack a sophisticated background in the behavioral sciences.

I hope that you will look into some of these or other publications on play and learning, and that this brief introduction has stimulated rather than satisfied your curiosity about the topic. If it has, you will find yourself pondering the questions, What is play? What good is play? and What is good play? again and again. And you will want to know more.